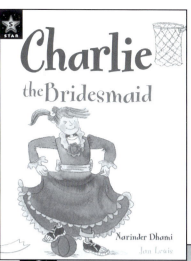

Charlie
the Bridesmaid

Narinder Dhami

Jan Lewis

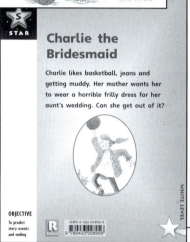

Charlie the Bridesmaid

Charlie likes basketball, jeans and getting muddy. Her mother wants her to wear a horrible frilly dress for her aunt's wedding. Can she get out of it?

OBJECTIVE
To predict story events and ending

ISBN 0-433-02895-5
9 780433 028956

WHITE LEVEL

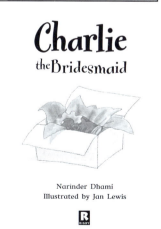

Charlie
the Bridesmaid

Narinder Dhami
Illustrated by Jan Lewis

RIGBY

The front cover

Read the title.

Does Charlie look like a bridesmaid? Why not?

What kind of girl is Charlie? What does the name Charlie suggest?

Generate words that might describe her character. What clues does the picture give you about Charlie?

The back cover

The blurb on the back cover gives us clues about the story.

What do you think Charlie does to get out of wearing a frilly bridesmaid's dress?

The title page

Can you guess what might be in the box?

Why is it wrapped up like that?

Read the author's and illustrator's names.

Lesson 1 (Chapter 1)

READ

Read pages 2 to 4

Purpose: To find out what Charlie's surprise was.

PAUSE

Pause at page 4

What is Charlie doing on page 2? What is she wearing?

How do we know she was looking forward to opening the package? (*Charlie got even more excited when she saw it!*)

What was the surprise?

Why do you think she didn't want to be a bridesmaid?

Can you find a phrase that tells us how Charlie felt? (*Charlie's face fell*)

Can you think of any words for how Charlie might be feeling now? (*disappointed, upset*)

Chapter 1

Charlie was in the garden, playing basketball by herself. Her jeans were muddy, but Charlie didn't care. She didn't mind getting dirty.

Charlie ran up to the basket, and was just about to shoot when her mother called her.

"Charlie! I've got a surprise for you!"

Charlie was excited.

"Great! I wonder what it is," she thought, as she ran into the house.

There was a large, white box lying on the table. Charlie got even more excited when she saw it. She never got packages in the post.

"The bridal shop sent it," said Charlie's mother. "It's your bridesmaid's dress!"

"Oh." Charlie's face fell. She really didn't want to be a bridesmaid at her aunt's wedding.

READ

Read pages 5 to 7

Purpose: To find out whether Charlie and her mum like the dress.

PAUSE

Pause at page 7

What does Charlie think of the dress? How do we know from the text? (*felt sick, it's horrible,* etc.)

Does Charlie's mum agree with her? What does she say to tell you this? (*You look so pretty!*)

How might Charlie's mum be feeling? Does she really like the dress? Why is she trying to persuade Charlie to wear it?

Find two words that tell us how Charlie's mum is feeling. (*frowned, sharply*)

What do you think Charlie's mum means by 'What will Aunt Beth say?' Who is Aunt Beth?

"Go on, open it," said her mother.

Charlie looked inside the box and felt sick. The dress was purple, and it had frills all over it.

"It's _. . it's horrible!_" she gasped.

"Nonsense! It's lovely!" said her mother. "Now put it on and let's see how it looks."

Charlie made a face.

"Come on Charlie," said her mother. "No arguments, please."

Charlie went to her room, and came down with the dress on. She felt really stupid in it.

"There! You look so pretty!" said her mother.

"I look stupid!" Charlie said, "I'm not wearing it! No way!"

Her mother frowned. "What will Aunt Beth say?"

"I don't care!" Charlie yelled, as she pulled the dress off. "I hate it!"

"We'll talk about this later," said her mother, sharply. "Now take it up to your bedroom."

READ

Read pages 8 to 11

Purpose: To find out what Charlie does to solve
her problem.

PAUSE

Pause at page 11

What does Charlie do to solve her problem?

What is a jumble sale?

Look at page 8 for words that tell us that Charlie was
cross. (*stormed, silly dress*)

Charlie grabbed the bridesmaid's dress, and stormed out of the room. Why couldn't she wear her jeans to Aunt Beth's wedding instead of a silly dress?

Charlie was so angry, she wasn't looking where she was going. She tripped over a big plastic bag, which was lying in the hall. The bag was full of clothes.

Charlie's mother had sorted them out for a jumble sale that afternoon.

Suddenly Charlie had an idea. She pushed the dress into the bag, underneath all the other clothes, and ran upstairs.

Then Charlie's father came in, picked up the bag, and carried it out to the car. He drove off with the bag to the sale.

READ

Read pages 12 and 13

Purpose: To meet Aunt Beth.

PAUSE

Pause at page 13

What is Aunt Beth like? How do you think Charlie feels? How do we know Charlie is embarrassed? (*she blushed*)

Please turn to page 15 for Revisit and Respond activities.

Lesson 2 (Chapter 2)

RECAP

Recap lesson 1

What sort of girl is Charlie?

Does she want to be a bridesmaid at Aunt Beth's wedding?

What didn't she want to wear?

What did she do to solve her problem?

What will Aunt Beth think when she finds out?

READ

Read pages 14 to 15

Purpose: To find out whether Charlie changes her mind.

PAUSE

Pause at page 15

How have Charlie's feelings about the dress changed? What words describe this? (*rather guilty*)

What is Charlie's new plan?

Charlie felt very pleased with herself. Now she'd never see that horrible dress again!

Later that day Aunt Beth came over.

"Hello, Charlie," she said, giving her a hug. "This is for you."

And she gave Charlie a great new CD.

"Thanks Aunt Beth!" Charlie said.

Her aunt always brought her a present whenever she came to visit.

"Did you like your bridesmaid's dress?" Aunt Beth asked her.

Charlie blushed. "Oh, yes."

"Good." Her aunt smiled. "You'll be a beautiful bridesmaid!"

Charlie didn't know what to say.

"I can't wait for the wedding," said Aunt Beth. "It's going to be a wonderful day!"

Chapter 2

Charlie began to feel rather guilty about the dress. Aunt Beth would be very upset when she found out what Charlie had done. The wedding day wouldn't be so wonderful after all.

"Charlie, I'm going to the jumble sale," called her mother. "Do you want to come?"

"Yes, please!" Charlie said quickly. She had to try and get that dress back!

When Charlie and her mother arrived at the sale, there were lots of other people waiting to go in. Charlie was very worried. What if someone bought the bridesmaid's dress before she could get it back? Then everyone would find out what she'd done!

Jumble Sale
Today!
opening 3pm

READ

Read pages 16 to 19

Purpose: To find out whether she finds the dress.

PAUSE

Pause at page 19

Where does Charlie see the dress?

What do you think she will do? Discuss the options. (*tell her mum, wait to see if the woman buys it,* etc.)

How do you think she feels?

The sale began. There were lots of different stalls. Charlie ran around them all as fast as she could, but she couldn't see her dress. Maybe someone had already bought it!

Then she saw it! The dress was hanging on a rack with lots of other clothes, and a woman was looking through them.

Suddenly Charlie saw her pick the bridesmaid's dress out!

"How pretty. I'll take this," said the woman to the man behind the table.

"That's mine!" Charlie gasped.

The woman looked surprised. "No, it isn't! I saw it first!"

"Oh, please can I have it?" Charlie begged.

"If it's yours, why is it for sale?" asked the woman.

READ

Read pages 20 to 23

Purpose: To find out who bought the dress.

PAUSE

Pause at page 23

Who bought the dress?

Why didn't Charlie buy it? (*no money*)

Why do you think the woman bought it for her?

Find the word on page 23 which tells us how Charlie felt to get her dress back. (*gratefully*) Generate other words that tell us how she might have felt.

Charlie explained and the woman began
to laugh.

"Well, I think you need it more than I do!"
she said, and she gave Charlie the dress.

"Do you want to buy that?" the man
asked Charlie.

"Yes, but I haven't got any money!"
Charlie said.

"No money, no dress!" the man said.

He tried to pull the dress out of Charlie's
hands, but Charlie wouldn't let go.

She had to get that dress back!

20

21

"I'll buy it for you," the woman said kindly,
and she paid the man.

"Oh, thank you!" Charlie said gratefully.

"I hope you enjoy your aunt's wedding!"
said the woman with a smile.

22

23

Aunt Beth's wedding was a wonderful day. Everyone said Charlie looked lovely in her bridesmaid's dress.

But there was something they didn't know . . .

24

READ

Read to the end

Purpose: To find out what happened at the wedding.

PAUSE

Pause at page 24

How did the wedding go? What did everyone say about Charlie?

Read the last line of the book. What was it that people didn't know? (*jeans under the dress*)

What else did people not know?

After Reading

Revisit and Respond

Lesson 1

T Ask the children what they think will happen in the second half of the story.

T Discuss whether they think Charlie's idea was a good one. What are the problems with the idea?

T Ask them to predict what Mum, Aunt Beth and Dad might say when they find out. Record suggestions on the whiteboard.

W Generate words or expressions to describe what we have learned about Charlie so far (e.g. *tomboy, lively, likes jeans, has a temper*).

Revisit and Respond

Lesson 2

T Ask the children to discuss whether Charlie enjoyed the wedding. Why? Do you think Charlie ever told her mum the story of what really happened, or did she keep it a secret?

T Role-play a conversation between Mum and Aunt Beth where Mum is trying to explain why Charlie doesn't like the dress.

S Make a set of question cards, i.e. a card each for *Why, What, Where, When, How*. Use these as prompts for a role-play activity where one child plays Charlie and the other children ask her questions, e.g. 'Why didn't you like the dress?'

W Ask the children to add words to the list which describe Charlie. (*sorry, grateful*)

W Ask the children to make a word bank of useful wedding words (e.g. *church, registry office, reception, bouquet, beautiful, relatives*).

W Ask them to look through the book and make a list of synonyms (words that mean the same or similar) for 'lovely' (*wonderful, pretty, beautiful*). Can they think of any more words?